# GLOBAL WARMING

© Aladdin Books Ltd 1991

Designed and produced by
Aladdin Books Ltd
28 Percy Street
London W1P 9FF

First published in 1991
in Great Britain by
Franklin Watts Ltd
96 Leonard Street
London EC2A 4RH

A CIP catalogue record
for this book is
available from the
British Library

ISBN 0 7496 0412 3     Printed in Belgium

Front cover: The effects of drought on a cornfield in America.
Back cover: Storm damage in London after the hurricane of 1987.

The author, Alexander Peckham, is a writer and environmentalist. He heads a consultancy which specialises in the transfer of environmental information to business and industry.

The consultant, Brian Gardiner, is an atmospheric physicist in the Ice and Climate Division of the British Antarctic Survey. He was one of the three scientists who discovered the hole in the ozone layer.

Design: Rob Hillier, Andy Wilkinson
Editor: Jen Green
Picture researcher: Emma Krikler
Illustrator: Ron Hayward Associates

# Contents

# GLOBAL WARMING

## ALEXANDER PECKHAM

**Franklin Watts**

London : New York : Toronto : Sydney

# Introduction

In the last few years it seems that the weather is always in the news. Hardly a month goes by without some report of a freak hurricane, flood or heat wave. For the first time in 50 years it has snowed in the Syrian desert, while in the Alps snowless winters are becoming ominously regular. Droughts in America's corn belt have been the worst for 100 years and crops have been devastated. In 1988, Gilbert, the most powerful hurricane on record, flattened whole villages in the Caribbean. In Britain, violent storms have created unprecedented damage and in 1989 the country experienced the warmest winter ever recorded. By analysing temperature records from over 1,000 places around the world, American and British climate experts have shown that the 1980s was the warmest decade since records began and that the atmosphere has warmed by half a degree Celsius since 1900.

In the 1980s scientists began to suspect that this warming was due to changes in the composition of the atmosphere – changes that were not natural but human-made. There is now international consensus that warming linked to human activities poses a very real threat to climates around the world. The scale of action required to change our lifestyles presents an immense challenge. This book explores the causes of global warming, the impact of climatic change and the ways in which we should begin to tackle the problems that lie ahead.

◁ In Bangladesh in 1988 (left) the heaviest rains in living memory made over 30 million people homeless. Reports of freak weather conditions alert us to the potential dangers of global warming, though they do not in themselves prove conclusively that the Earth's thermostat is out of control.

# The Greenhouse Effect

The gas carbon dioxide makes up only a tiny fraction of our atmosphere, but without it, people, animals and plants would not be able to live on Earth. Carbon dioxide is the main heat-absorbing component in the atmosphere; it keeps the air at a temperature comfortable for life on Earth. Carbon dioxide and other heat-trapping gases in the atmosphere protect us from the cold of outer space, just as a greenhouse protects plants from winter frost. They are therefore called "greenhouse gases" and the warming effect they create is the "Greenhouse Effect".

▽ Rising sea levels are a major threat posed by global warming. As land ice melts and mountain glaciers and the huge ice caps of Greenland and Antarctica disappear, the water flowing from them will run into the sea. The oceans will expand as they warm, leading to danger of flooding worldwide.

Differences in the make-up of the atmosphere affect the temperature on planets in our solar system.

### Mars

Because Mars has a very thin atmosphere, its Greenhouse Effect is extremely weak. Mars' atmosphere absorbs so little energy from the Sun that the average temperature is minus 100°C – far too cold for life to exist.

### Earth

The atmosphere around the Earth is made up of 78 per cent nitrogen, 21 per cent oxygen and only 0.03 per cent carbon dioxide. This balance keeps the air temperature at an average 15°C, exactly right to support life.

### Venus

On Venus, a thick atmosphere made up mostly of carbon dioxide traps so much heat that the average temperature is almost 500°C. This fiery inferno battered by fierce winds is definitely not hospitable to life.

By leading a lifestyle which increases the amount of greenhouse gases in the atmosphere, scientists believe we are intensifying the Greenhouse Effect. They predict this will lead to global warming – the term applied to the heating of the atmosphere. Global warming threatens to change the forces that control climate. Although climates have varied in the past, this has been due to factors like natural changes in the tilt of the Earth – not because of human-made damage. How will climate change affect life on Earth? During the last ice age vast areas of northern Europe and North America were covered by thick ice. Yet at the depths of this ice age, the average temperature was only 5°C colder than today.

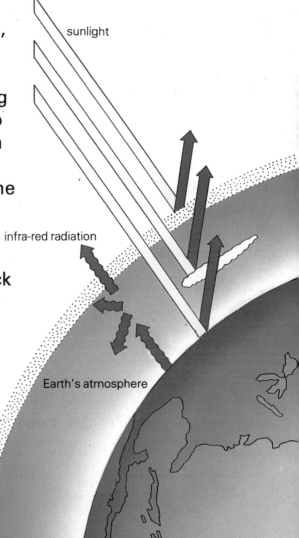

sunlight

infra-red radiation

Earth's atmosphere

▷ Much of the light from the Sun that reaches our planet is reflected back into space by the atmosphere, clouds and the Earth. The Earth's surface absorbs energy from sunlight and later releases it as infra-red radiation; some of this is absorbed by the greenhouse gases in the atmosphere, keeping temperatures right for life.

# Shifting balance

Until about 150 years ago, the balance of gases in the atmosphere had not changed much for thousands of years. In the last century and a half, however, the air's natural balance has been disturbed. By burning fossil fuels (coal, gas and oil) to generate increasing amounts of energy, we release more and more carbon dioxide, the most important greenhouse gas. There is now ten per cent more carbon dioxide in the atmosphere than there was 30 years ago. When tropical forests are cut and the wood is burned or allowed to rot, carbon dioxide also escapes into the air. The carbon dioxide we are releasing accounts for more than half of global warming.

◁ Like other plants, rainforest trees absorb carbon dioxide and help maintain the balance of oxygen in the air. When the forest is destroyed the carbon dioxide is released again.

Chlorofluorocarbons (CFCs), the gases responsible for damaging the ozone layer, are also greenhouse gases. Used in the manufacture of aerosol sprays and refrigerators, every molecule of CFC is an alarming 10,000 times more effective at trapping heat than one molecule of carbon dioxide. Methane, a gas used for cooking and heating, is another important greenhouse gas. It escapes from many different sources: leaking gas pipelines, rotting rubbish, paddy fields and from the world's 1,500 million cattle. Slowly but surely, as greenhouse gases increase, the invisible balance that has nurtured life for thousands of years is destroyed.

▽ From the exhausts of cars, buses, lorries and ships, and from the chimneys of factories and power stations, carbon dioxide pours into the atmosphere – billions of tonnes of it every year.

▽ Human-made greenhouse gases contribute in varying degrees to global warming. Carbon dioxide, from the combustion of fossil fuels and from the destruction of the rainforests, is by far the most important. But even small amounts of CFCs create a great deal of warming, and methane and nitrous oxide also add to the problem.

Carbon dioxide 55%

CFCs 24%

Nitrous oxide 6%

Methane 15%

# Changing climates

The forces that drive climate are very complicated. It has been difficult for researchers to prove that global warming is a reality, and work out how our lifestyles might be affected. The Intergovernmental Panel on Climate Change (IPCC) was set up to try to resolve this uncertainty. IPCC scientists are now convinced that unless emissions of greenhouse gases are reduced, average temperatures will rise faster during the next century than at any time since the end of the last ice age. Some places will become drier and others wetter, and although most places will get hotter, a few could become cooler.

The IPCC, a special committee of climate experts from around the world, was set up in 1988 to investigate the threat of global warming. Their task was a hard one; with the most powerful computers available, meteorologists find it difficult enough to forecast the daily weather, let alone predict climate change over the next few decades. IPCC scientists have now "calculated with certainty" that the Earth will get warmer if action is not taken immediately.

▽ In Africa droughts may become more frequent as a result of global warming.

The impact of climate change could be drastic. Tropical storms will become more common. Plants and animals that find it difficult to adapt could die out. As temperatures rise, diseases now found only in the tropics may become common. Ice caps and glaciers will melt and the oceans will expand as they warm. The IPCC calculates that half a million kilometres of coastline could be flooded. If that happens, many islands would simply drown. A sea level rise of just a metre could turn island states like the Maldives in the Indian Ocean into uninhabitable swamps.

### The impact of drought
Central North America has been called the bread basket of the world; this grain-producing area aims to export 120 million tonnes of grain a year to feed people in places as far apart as the Soviet Union, Africa and Asia. But in the 1980s repeated droughts in the area reduced world grain stocks to a record low. The IPCC predicts that the region could continue to experience drought as temperatures rise and rainfall decreases; this could lead to famine in many countries. The United States will not be alone in this adversity; many other areas will experience repeated droughts and crop failure.

△ Disastrous floods like this one in the Sudan in East Africa will become more common as global warming takes hold.

# The impact of change

▽ Food, water, shelter and basic amenities have to be provided for refugees like this Sudanese woman, but the countries to which refugees flee are often very poor themselves and have little to spare. Today there are already about 14 million refugees around the world, but this figure could rise steeply as a result of global warming.

Flooded coastlines, violent storms, droughts, disease, the possible extinction of plant and animal species – these things can hardly fail to affect how people live around the world. In the past, famines caused by drought and pests have caused great hardship. When there is no food, people are forced to abandon their homes and become refugees. This causes widespread suffering and places a great burden on the areas that refugees move to. One region that could suffer horribly is Egypt, where a sea level rise would flood a large expanse of land in the fertile Nile Delta. Enclosed by the sea to the north and by deserts on other sides, the people will have nowhere to move to. Before the end of the next century, sea levels may rise by as much as a metre, so the problem is very real.

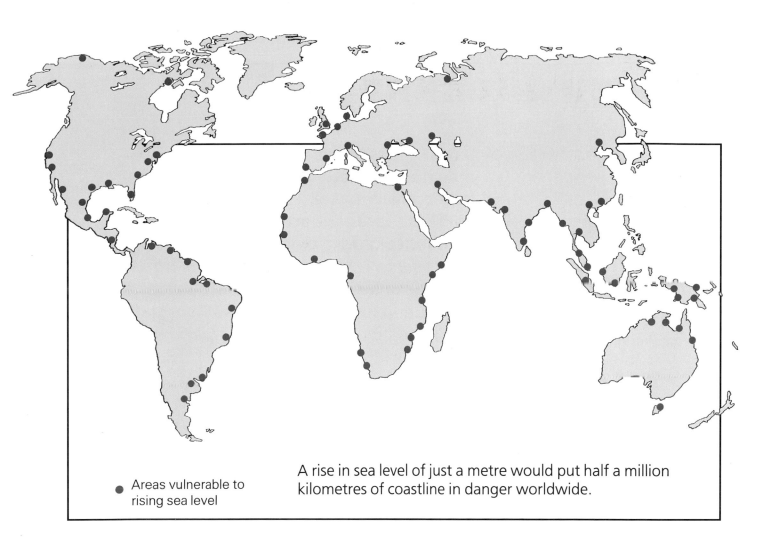

A rise in sea level of just a metre would put half a million kilometres of coastline in danger worldwide.

● Areas vulnerable to rising sea level

If people are forced to move to areas where life is already harsh, conflicts with local people and political instability are possible. As wild plants and trees die, the situation could become even worse: millions of farmers depend on plants and grasses to feed their animals. Healthy forests are equally vital to the two thousand million people in the world who use wood for fuel. Global warming will also affect water supplies. Growing cities like Lima in Peru already place great strain on local water resources, and global warming would make such shortages much more serious. Even in developed regions like northern Europe, climate change would devastate present finely balanced agricultural patterns.

◁ Crowds flee flood-hit areas in Bangladesh in 1988. A one-metre rise in the sea level could flood 14 per cent of Bangladesh's farmland and displace millions of people.

# Energy dilemma

Carbon dioxide released by burning fossil fuels makes up 40 per cent of the greenhouse gases humans pour into the atmosphere. Recent estimates suggest that the 20,000 million tonnes of carbon dioxide currently released into the atmosphere each year will have to be cut by more than 60 per cent if global warming is to be halted. In industrial countries we depend on fossil fuels to provide us with the energy to heat and air-condition our offices and homes, to run our cars and our electrical appliances. Huge amounts of energy are needed to manufacture goods like dish washers, videos and microwaves. The energy-intensive lifestyle we lead is echoed by the amount of carbon dioxide we produce.

The only practical ways of controlling carbon dioxide emissions are to develop energy sources that don't burn fossil fuels and produce no greenhouse gases, and to make better use of the energy that we do produce. Huge savings can be made in homes, offices and factories by using more energy-efficient appliances, and by making use of the waste heat produced by power stations and factories. Improvements in public transport would also help by reducing fuel consumption.

So far there are few signs of these changes taking place. Industrialised countries have become used to using huge amounts of cheap fossil fuels and will go to almost any lengths to protect supplies. There has been very little real effort to develop clean energy sources like the sun, wind and waves, which will not run out.

▷ Energy is taken for granted in the West; draping lights round desert cacti looks pretty, but is it a waste of energy? The United States uses about a quarter of the world's energy. Each year it pumps ten times more carbon dioxide into the atmosphere than all the countries in Africa combined.

△ Agriculture is becoming increasingly energy-intensive. Nitrogenous fertilisers are one example. In the last forty years the consumption of fertilisers has risen steeply. It takes about one tonne of oil to produce enough energy to make one tonne of fertilisers. That means that more than the equivalent of 100,000,000 tonnes of oil are used every year just to make fertilisers.

▷ Although these cars are not getting anywhere very fast, they are burning significant amounts of fuel and contributing to global warming. The average car in the United States still only manages about 12 km per litre, when it could easily be designed to go twice as far on the same amount.

# The development dilemma

There is a huge difference between the amount of energy used in the industrialised countries and in the developing ones. The richer nations, with only one quarter of the world's population, consume about three quarters of the world's energy. On average, each individual in the West uses 80 times more energy than each African person. This isn't surprising – very few people in developing countries have cars and most don't even have electricity in their homes.

But today people in the developing nations want more of these material comforts, and their energy use is growing fast. If the whole of the world's population were to depend on fossil fuels as industrialised countries do today, three times more carbon dioxide would be released into the atmosphere each year.

▽ Paddy fields such as these ones on steep slopes in the Philippines are a major source of methane. As the world's human population has rocketed, so has the area covered by paddy fields for growing rice. Methane emissions currently contribute about 15 per cent to global warming. Because the gas is produced by the farming on which millions depend for food, tackling this aspect of the problem is going to be very difficult.

△ As countries develop economically and populations grow, more pressure is placed on available land. Carbon dioxide is released as forests are cut. As farmlands expand and cattle herds like this one on a plateau in Nigeria grow larger, more methane is produced – adding even more greenhouse gases to the atmosphere.

Another side of the dilemma is population. World population is now just over five billion, but by 2025 it could top eight billion. The developing world could soon produce four times as much carbon dioxide as developed nations do today – a situation that would be suicidal for us all. As the world's population grows, pressure on land increases; forests are cut for timber, firewood and to make way for farmland, and more carbon dioxide is added to the air. These trends are hard to reverse. As American and European economies developed during the last century, our populations grew very fast; forests were cut and uncultivated lands ploughed up. Is it fair for us to ask the developing world not to do the same?

World population is currently just over five billion, and is still rising. If we continue to use the same amount of energy per person, by 2025 we will have to increase world fuel consumption by 60 per cent. Growing populations need more land to grow food, causing methane emissions to rise.

1990: 5 billion

1075: 4 billion

1930: 2 billion

1850: 1 billion

△ Cyclists on a street in Wuxi, China. If people in China abandoned their bicycles in favour of cars, the environment would suffer and global warming would occur even faster. While so many people in industrialised nations have cars, it is difficult to argue that those in developing countries should not own them too.

# A call for action

### Exhausting energy

The energy required to build and run a car is vast. In the United States alone, about fourteen billion litres of petrol are burned by cars every year and the World Watch Institute in California has calculated that the world's 400 million cars release more than 500 tonnes of carbon dioxide into the atmosphere every year, contributing enormously to the problem of global warming. There are presently about 1.8 people to every car in the United States – in China there are 1,370. The number of cars in the world would more than double if the Chinese were to own cars on the same scale as the North Americans. It will simply not be possible for everyone in the world to own a car; if they did, the environmental impact would be catastrophic.

All countries produce greenhouse gases, and all will suffer as a result of global warming. It is in every nation's interest that international agreement and action are arranged as quickly as possible to tackle the problem. In recent years, such co-operation between nations has begun to happen. In the face of growing evidence that the ozone layer is being destroyed by CFCs, many nations signed the Montreal Protocol in 1987 and agreed to phase out ozone-destroying chemicals. This agreement sets an example for the kind of international action needed to reduce the emission of gases like carbon dioxide. But developing an agreement to reduce greenhouse gas emissions will be far harder, as energy plays a crucial role in economic development.

▽ So far issues like acid rain and ozone depletion have attracted more demonstrations than global warming. We can identify what is responsible for withered forests and the hole in the ozone layer, but it is harder to blame hurricanes, droughts and floods on global warming.

STOP ACID POLLUTION NOW !

At a meeting on the changing atmosphere in Toronto in 1988, scientists and politicians from around the world identified global warming as a problem "second only to nuclear war". Calls for international action are increasing. The European Community believes that a "global response should be made without further delay." In the United States, the Union of Concerned Scientists sent a petition signed by 40 Nobel prizewinners to President Bush asking him to take immediate action. Much depends on carrying out the decisions made at the World Climate Conference in Geneva in November 1990, where the IPCC's findings were discussed by many prominent politicians and scientists. There is a great need for an effective international convention to control greenhouse gas emissions.

**CFCs**
Invented in the 1920s, CFCs are pumped into aerosol cans, used to blow the bubbles in foam furniture, as cleaning agents in industry and to make refrigerators (below) and air conditioners work. But because of the damage they cause to the ozone layer, governments have now agreed to phase them out. Putting a stop to CFC use will help save the ozone layer, and also reduce global warming.

◁ International co-operation will be needed to halt global warming.

# Words and deeds

Echoing public worries, many politicians have been voicing concern about global warming. The environment has become an important topic for politicians seeking election. For example, during the 1988 presidential campaign in the United States, George Bush announced his intention "to do something about the Greenhouse Effect". But it's one thing to acknowledge the gravity of the problem and another to act. So far attempts to reach an international agreement to limit carbon dioxide emissions have failed. At a conference on the environment at Bergen, Norway in 1990, most industrialised nations confirmed it would be possible to stabilise emissions by the end of the century. But the United States, Britain, Canada and the Soviet Union were amongst nations who blocked an actual agreement to do so.

Levels of carbon dioxide in the atmosphere, shown in parts per million, are measured at Mauna Loa Observatory in Hawaii. Seasonal variations are caused by the growth and decay of vegetation in the northern hemisphere.

1960          1965          1970

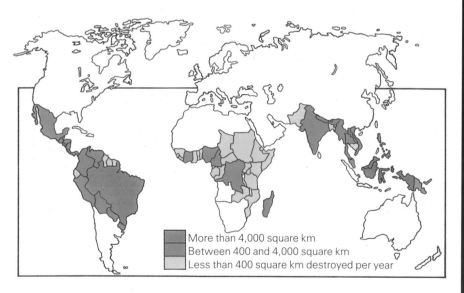

More than 4,000 square km
Between 400 and 4,000 square km
Less than 400 square km destroyed per year

△ Vast areas of tropical forest are destroyed every year. It is vital to protect what remains and ensure that further cutting is balanced by replanting on an organised basis.

▷ Bringing living conditions in shanty towns like this one in Bombay up to Western standards would increase the level of carbon dioxide in the atmosphere.

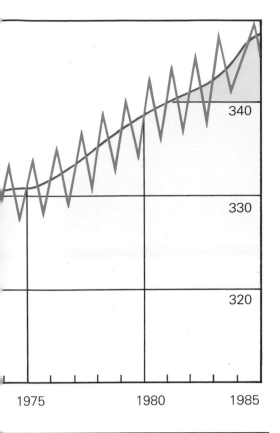

340

330

320

1975          1980          1985

Energy-intensive countries like the United States are worried that reduced fossil fuel consumption would damage their economies. These countries emphasise the scientific uncertainties of global warming and claim that more evidence is needed before action can be taken. But despite the lack of international consensus, some countries have already begun to act. Japan plans to stabilise greenhouse gas emissions at ten per cent above present levels. Other countries have set more impressive targets: Germany and New Zealand have resolved to reduce carbon dioxide emissions by 25 per cent before 2005, and the Dutch government is committed to reducing emissions by eight per cent before the end of the century.

▽ The New York skyline has come to represent modern, energy-intensive living.

It will require radical restructuring for the United States to lower its fossil fuel use enough to halt global warming.

# People power

Individuals and groups of people can play a vital part in the fight against global warming. In the industrialised nations, pressure groups like Greenpeace and Friends of the Earth have helped to make us aware of the dangers of global warming. They also campaign to promote energy efficiency and renewable energy technologies. As yet, however, there are few signs that individuals are doing much to reduce the amount of greenhouse gases they produce, though we could all do a great deal. Simple measures like insulating houses, using energy-efficient equipment and travelling by public transport can dramatically reduce our energy use. In Britain, the average household is responsible for about 20 tonnes of carbon dioxide every year. With 25 million households in the country, if everyone took action the savings would be enormous.

△ The Centre of Alternative Technology in Wales is a living community which proves that Western lifestyles can be adapted to use resources more sensibly. It uses very little energy and almost all from renewable resources.

▽ Amazon Indian leaders protest against a proposed hydroelectric scheme. Many groups campaigning to defend traditional ways of life like these South American Indians are indirectly fighting global warming. The lifestyles they defend are not energy-intensive and involve preserving forest resources such as fruits and medicines.

In 1985 the Greenpeace ship *Rainbow Warrior* was bombed by the French secret service in Auckland harbour, New Zealand. Those who challenge the status quo sometimes meet with violence from their opponents. Chico Mendes, the leader of Brazil's rubber tappers, was shot and killed in December 1988 because he opposed the rich landowners and cattle ranchers who were destroying the rainforest. Undeterred by threats, groups around the world continue to call for change.

◁ The Chipco movement has saved many trees. In the early 1970s women in the High Himalayas stopped trees from being felled by commercial loggers by hugging them and refusing to let go. The protests spread all over India and the national government was compelled to ban logging on hillsides over 1,000 metres. Now the Chipco movement is also involved in forestry management.

In the developing world most people are poor and have more immediate worries than global warming. Some people, however, are helping to solve the problem. In many countries small groups have formed to fight the destruction of the local environments on which they depend. For example, many groups are fighting to save the forests in which they live and whose destruction produces greenhouse gases. Such protestors have often made enemies, some of whom are prepared to use violence to achieve their objectives.

# Priorities

Controlling carbon dioxide emissions and getting rid of CFCs are only two elements in the fight against global warming. Population is also one of the most urgent priorities. The population explosion worldwide must be addressed immediately. Increasing numbers of people put more and more pressure on the land. So the population explosion is accelerating the rate at which greenhouse gases, like methane from agriculture and carbon dioxide from forest destruction, are released into the atmosphere. Although the need to control population growth is very urgent, the problem has not been given the attention it deserves. So far, few attempts to limit the size of families have had much impact. It is difficult to introduce birth control in countries where traditionally, large families with many children are seen as a blessing.

Transport accounts for about 20 per cent of the human-made Greenhouse Effect, but this amount could be cut down greatly if public transport was used more. A car burns far more energy per passenger than a train or bus. A double decker bus, for example, uses about 80 per cent less energy per passenger than a car. It is vitally important that we invest in public transport now. Of course, there will also be the added benefits of less pollution, congestion and much safer streets.

▽ Public transport systems like this one in Jaiselmer, India, offer the opportunity to save fuel and reduce carbon dioxide emissions.

▽ Family planning campaigns like this one in China often make use of advertising. They need to become even more effective if they are to help slow the population explosion.

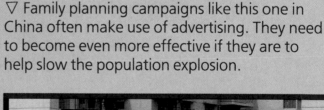

▽ An oil palm plantation in Cameroon, West Africa, stretches towards the distant rainforest. Trees contain many useful resources like nuts, resins and medicines. If forests are managed properly and markets for forest products developed, they can provide a continuing livelihood for forest people. Developing countries don't always have the money to invest in protecting the rainforests. Industrial nations will have to help pay for the protection of resources like forests which are important to people all around the world.

Forests are another extremely important priority. The destruction of forests, particularly in tropical and equatorial regions, pumps large amounts of carbon dioxide into the atmosphere. This devastation must be halted, and ways found of helping people to make a living from forests without destroying them.

Trees absorb carbon dioxide as they grow. Planting trees is therefore one way of absorbing some of the excess carbon dioxide in the air. Some countries have promised to plant lots of trees. In particular, Australia's prime minister, Bob Hawke, has promised to plant one billion trees by the end of the century – that means planting about 300,000 a day until then. It would take a new forest the size of France to be planted every year to absorb the extra carbon dioxide we are pumping into the atmosphere.

# Investing in the future

Energy from the sun, running water, waves, tides and wind can be harnessed without producing greenhouse gases. These types of energy have the added advantage that, unlike fossil fuels, they are renewable; the wind will always blow, the tides always rise and fall and the Sun's rays always beat down onto the Earth. Of the renewable energy sources, power from running water like rivers or the outflow from dams (hydropower) is already used on a large scale. A number of promising designs to harness wave energy have been put forward, but none have yet gone beyond the experimental stage. One design from Scotland called the "Nodding Duck" was stopped because the British government greatly over-estimated the cost of the scheme.

A British project to harness tidal energy involves the building of a barrage across the river Severn estuary to trap the tidal energy there. The scheme could eventually produce about 8,500 megawatts of power – the equivalent of four coal-fired power stations or over 2,000 huge windmills. The principles involved in barrage-building are simple. As the tide rises and falls, water is forced through pipes in the barrage, driving huge turbines and generating electricity. But it would cost an estimated £8 billion to build the 20 kilometre barrage.

▽ Solar panels, which use water to trap the Sun's heat, are already used in homes around the world.

The Sun's rays can also be used to generate electricity, but as yet, this technology is too expensive for general use.

Windmills designed to capture energy from the wind and turn it into electricity are now highly efficient and can produce up to four megawatts each – enough to power 40,000 100-watt light bulbs. Solar energy is already used in many countries, but there is enormous potential for expanding this energy supply. So far, there is only one large tidal power station in the world, at La Rance in France, but a number of other schemes have been designed.

Experts don't agree how much energy can be harvested from renewable energy sources, but they believe that it will take a long time to develop the supply. The sooner we start investing seriously in the technology needed, the sooner we will put a stop to global warming.

Nuclear power makes use of energy locked up in atoms to generate electricity. The processes involved do not produce greenhouse gases and do not add to global warming. Nuclear technology has been developed and already provides a significant amount of energy. But nuclear power can be dangerous. Accidents have already happened, most recently at Chernobyl in the Soviet Union in 1986. Properly managed, nuclear energy holds immense potential to meet energy needs around the world.

▽ Wind farms like this one in California contain hundreds of windmills and produce significant amounts of electricity. Such schemes help reduce dependence on fossil fuels and are being developed in North America and Europe.

# Technofixes

A number of technical solutions have been proposed to counteract global warming. Unfortunately these schemes are quite unrealistic with today's technology. But if science can't cure the problem, it will be useful in helping to deal with the side-effects. As sea levels rise we will need defences to protect coastal areas worldwide from erosion and flooding, but these will be very expensive. If we manage to keep the sea at bay, humans will still have to rely heavily on technology to solve other problems.

The Thames barrier in London was not designed to cope with the level of flooding which global warming could bring. It will need to be heightened to cope with rising sea levels. In Britain government advisers estimate that it would cost £8 billion to build defences along the coast against a one and a half metre rise in sea level.

The technology needed to protect coastlines and fight the effects of global warming will be costly. It will stretch the resources of many countries, particularly in the developing world. The lion's share of the funding should be met by the industrialised nations who are responsible for having caused most of the problem.

Biotechnology is likely to play a vital role in food production as farmers search for new plant breeds to withstand changing climates. Water from wet areas may have to be pumped through complex pipe networks to cities whose water supplies have dried up. Buildings will have to be designed to cope with extreme weather conditions. There will be no easy solutions, and even if humans are successful in controlling greenhouse gas emissions, some warming is already incvitable. The world will have to brace itself for unpredictable changes.

Traditional housing on stilts in Singapore may provide inspiration for architects around the world faced with problems of repeated flooding caused by global warming. The modern technology which has been developed in countries like the Netherlands, where much of the country is actually below sea level, will also prove useful.

# Gas facts

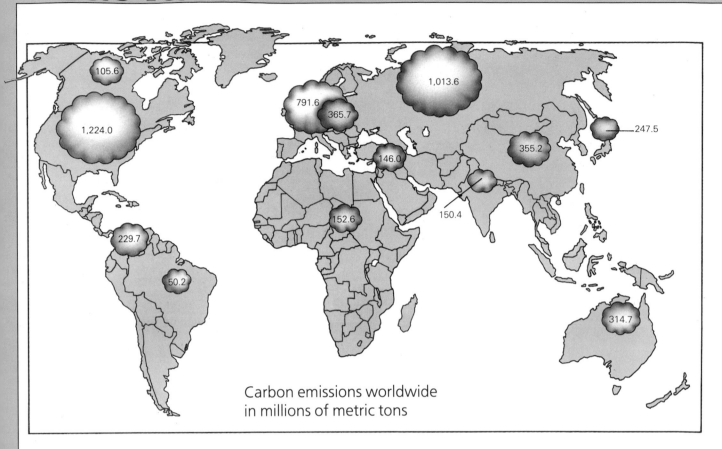

Carbon emissions worldwide
in millions of metric tons

By analysing bubbles of air trapped in snowfall and buried in the ice in Antarctica, scientists have been able to assess the changes that have taken place in the composition of the atmosphere. They have discovered that there is now about 26 per cent more carbon dioxide in the air than at the beginning of the industrial revolution in the mid-eighteenth century. In the same period the amount of methane in the atmosphere has increased by more than 200 per cent.

CFCs were invented in the 1920s and are used in industry. All the CFCs in the atmosphere have therefore been put there by humans in the last 70 years.

Measurements taken in recent years show that the concentration of carbon dioxide in the atmosphere is increasing at about 0.05 per cent a year. Methane concentrations are increasing even faster, at almost one per cent a year, and levels of CFCs have been growing at about four per cent a year.

Scientists have calculated the reductions required to stabilise the concentration of human-made greenhouse gases at present levels. They believe that carbon dioxide emissions need to be reduced by more than 60 per cent, methane by 20 per cent, nitrous oxide by 80 per cent and CFCs by 80 per cent.

Not all greenhouse gases have the same potential to trap heat. CFCs are at least 10,000 times stronger as greenhouse gases than carbon dioxide, methane is 30 times stronger and nitrous oxide is 150 times stronger.

Responding to evidence that CFCs are destroying the ozone layer, many countries have agreed to phase them out. At the rate CFCs were being pumped into the atmosphere they would soon have overtaken carbon dioxide as the main cause of global warming. A great deal still has to be done to ensure that the chemicals introduced to replace them are not themselves also greenhouse gases.

## Chronology

**1827** The French mathematician Baron Jean Baptist Fourier first suggests that the atmosphere might play an important role in trapping energy from the Sun.

**1863** British scientist John Tyndall describes how water vapour in the atmosphere helps to keep the world warm.

**1896** The Swedish chemist Svante Arrhenius suggests that the carbon dioxide added to the air by burning coal could make the atmosphere warmer.

**1957** International geophysical year – involves more than 30,000 scientists and 1,000 research stations. The year marks the turning point in climatic research and the establishment of atmospheric monitoring stations at the South Pole and on the Mauna Loa volcano in Hawaii.

**1970s** Energy analysts predict a large increase in the use of fossil fuels and that this will cause the level of carbon dioxide in the air to double in a short space of time. Governments begin to fund research.

**1980s** Concern mounts internationally amongst members of the public, scientists and politicians as more climatic disasters strike around the globe.

**1985** Scientists from 29 industrial nations meet at Villach in Austria to review current research into the Greenhouse Effect. They conclude that the threat is very real.

**1986** Scientists at the Climatic Research Unit at the University of East Anglia produce evidence that global temperatures have risen half a degree Celsius over the last century.

**1988** As a result of growing concern, the Intergovernmental Panel on Climate Change is established, pooling the knowledge of climate experts around the globe.

**1988** Results from the Mauna Loa atmospheric monitoring station show that the level of carbon dioxide in the air increased by over ten per cent between 1958 and 1988, providing convincing evidence that humankind is indeed wreaking huge changes upon the atmosphere.

**1988** The warmest year ever recorded. The decade 1978 – 1988 is also the warmest ever recorded.

**1990** The Intergovernmental Panel on Climate Change reports that there is now certainty that interference with the atmosphere will cause global warming.

## Glossary

**Atmosphere** A mixed layer of gases (mainly nitrogen and oxygen) which surrounds the Earth. These gases are concentrated in the lower atmosphere which stretches up to 10 km above the Earth's surface.

**Climate** The pattern of weather averaged over a long time. Weather can change from hour to hour but changes in climate are measured over decades and centuries.

**Fossil fuels** Fuel composed of fossilised remnants of plants and micro-organisms. Coal, gas and oil are fossil fuels.

**Greenhouse Effect** The process by which certain gases (greenhouse gases) in the Earth's atmosphere trap heat from the Sun, keeping the planet's surface warm enough for life.

**Global warming** The result of people adding greenhouse gases to the atmosphere so that it traps more heat.

**Ozone layer** A layer of the atmosphere at a height between 15 and 30 km above the Earth's surface which contains a high concentration of ozone. This layer filters out harmful ultra-violet radiation from the Sun, preventing it from reaching the Earth's surface.

# Index

## Photographic Credits

Cover and pages 10-11 top and bottom, 11, 12, 12-13, 19 left and 22 bottom left: Topham Picture Source; pages 4-5, 23 and 24 right: Frank Spooner Pictures; pages 6, 7 left and right, 8-9, 14-15, 16-17, 27 and 29 inset: Zefa; page 7 middle: NASA; pages 8-9 inset and 19 right: The Environmental Picture Library; pages 15 left, 16, 17 and 21: J. Allan Cash Photo Library; page 15 right: Robert Harding Picture Library; pages 18, 20-21 and 25: Hutchinson Library; page 22 top: The Centre for Alternative Technology, Machynlleth; page 22 bottom right: Panos Pictures; pages 24 left and 28-29: Spectrum Colour Library; page 26: A.E.R.E Harwell.